LIVE
L🐾VE
PURRR

— For Pepe & Mika. —

Find Cranky Cat! - Search Fun For Cat Lovers
© JBroecker Books, 2019 (Cambridge, UK)

Published by JBroecker Books
info@JBroeckerBooks.com
Visit the author's website at www.JBroeckerBooks.com

Picture credit: All images were modified for the purpose of this book and are used under a premium license from freepik (www.freepik.com) or shutterstock (www.shutterstock.com). The artists of the original illustrations are: GDJ/openclipart.org (p. 5), Marianna Pashchuk (p. 7), Elsystudio (p. 9 and Bonus p. 2), pingvin_house (p. 11), Natkacheva (p. 13), 9george (p. 15), freepik (p. 17), jsabirova (p. 19), tets (p. 21), Dinara Yumatova (p. 23), and hollymolly/Vecteezy.com (p. 25, front/back cover, Bonus ps. 2 and 3).

Find Cranky Cat! - Search Fun For Cat Lovers
Copyright © 2019 Jana Broecker
1st Edition, 2019
ISBN 978-1-912683-00-0 (eBook)
ISBN 978-1-912683-02-4 (Paperback)
JBroecker Books, 2019 (Cambridge, UK)

ISBN 9781912683024

JBroeckerBooks

Find
Cranky Cat!

SEARCH FUN FOR
CAT LOVERS

2 Ways To Play:

Easy:

Choose Cranky Cat!

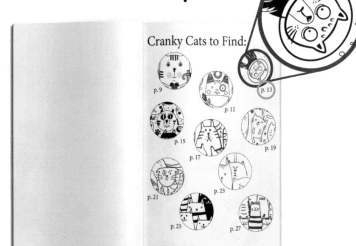

Find Cranky Cat!

Difficult:

Do not look!

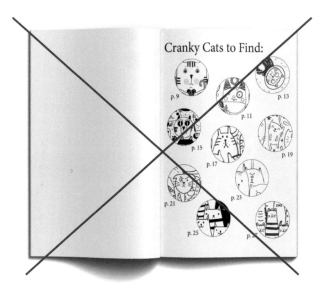

Find Cranky Cat!

Cranky Cats To Find:

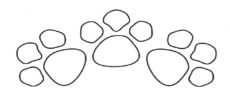

"**Cats** rule the **world** ."

James Davis
Garfield Cartoonist

Difficulty: 🐾🐾🐾🐾🐾

"One **cat** just leads
to ANOTHER."

Ernest Hemingway
American Writer

Difficulty: 🐾🐾🐾🐾🐾

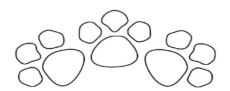

"To **err** is *human,*
to PURR is feline."

Robert Byrne
American Writer

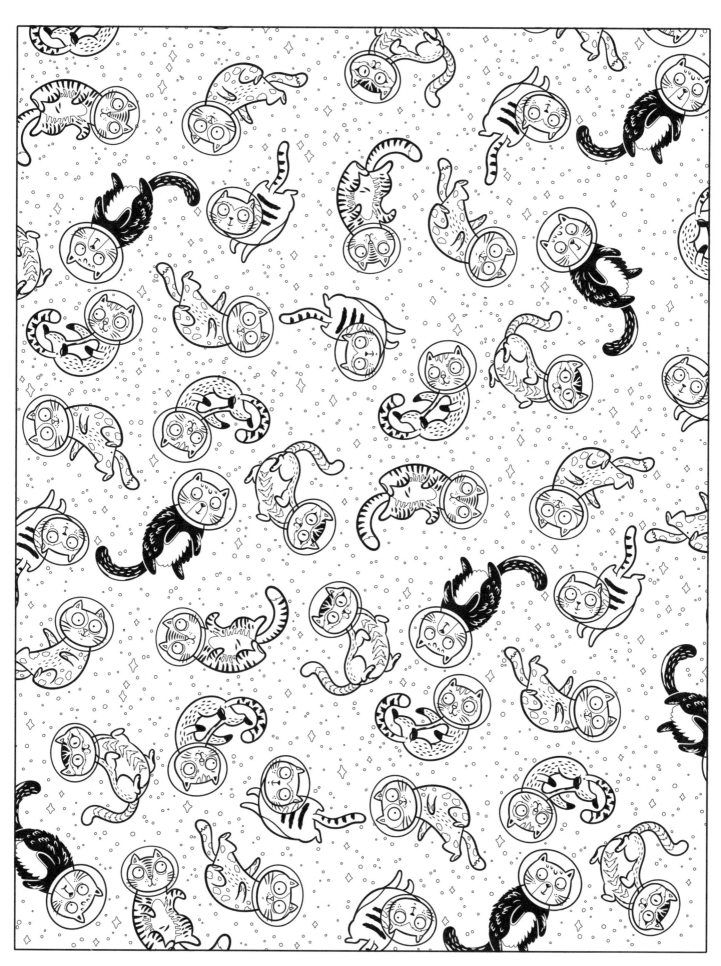

"**Cats** choose **us;**
we **don't**
own them."

Kristin Cast
American Writer

14

"Time spent with a **cat** is never **wasted**."

Sidonie-Gabrielle Colette
French Writer

"What greater **gift** than **the** *love* OF a CAT."

Charles Dickens
British Writer

18

Difficulty: 🐾🐾🐾

"A **dog** will flatter **you,** but YOU HAVE **to flatter** the **cat**."

George Mikes
British Writer

"Cats **randomly** refuse to follow **orders** to prove they **can**."

Ilona & Andrew Gordon
American Writers

"In **ancient** times, cats *were* WORSHIPPED as **GODS**; **THEY** have not forgotten **this.**"

Terry Pratchett
British Writer

"There **should** always *be* **one** MORE cat than **PERSON,** *so* everyone **HAS** one to **pet,** and **I have** two **myself.**"

Jarod Kintz
American Writer

Difficulty: 🐾🐾🐾

27

"A *happy* arrangement:
Many people prefer **CATS**
ᴛᴏ other **people**,
and many **cats**
prefer people
to other **cats**."

Mason Cooley
American Aphorist

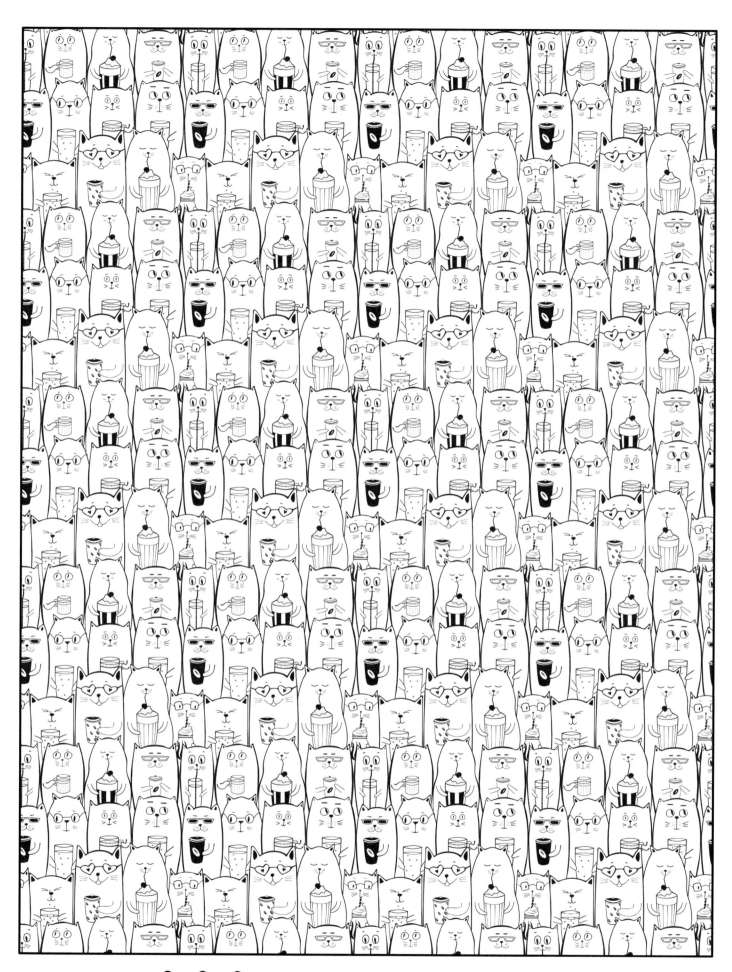

"I **have** found *it* is surprisingly DIFFICULT TO remain *sad* when **a** cat **is** doing **its** level BEST to sandpaper *one's* **cheeks**."

Robin Lorraine LaFevers
American Writer

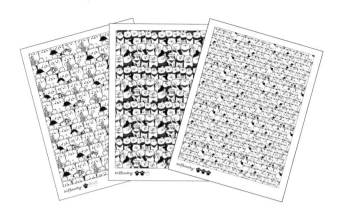

For the dog lover in your life

Why not get **FREE** access to **3 Bonus Pages**?

Download your **Find Cranky Cat Freebie**:
www.jbroeckerbooks.com/freebies/
or scan the QR code.

About The Author

Dr. Jana Broecker is a Senior Scientist and the mom of two during the day and an independent author of picture books at night. She is originally from Germany, has lived in four countries and two continents, throws the longest birthday party EVERY year (as does her twin), and has the best new ideas when driving a car (on either side of the road). She and her family share their home in Sawston, UK, with Boris Handsome, the cat, and an impressive collection of children's books.

How To Get In Touch?

JBroeckerBooks.com
info@jbroeckerbooks.com

Picture Books With A Twist

@janabroecker

JB: @author.janabroecker
SL: @liutaart

If you enjoyed this book, please leave a review on Amazon to support my small business and me as an independent artist and author. Thank you!

love, Jana

You Might Also Like:

Pilot Ray - Dream BIG Series

Tiny snail Ray has one dream, and that is to fly! Will he prove that you can achieve BIG things, no matter how small you are? An adventure book series about **believing in yourself** and the **importance of family and friends.**

A Million Years From Home

A frozen dinosaur egg thaws in today's Africa. Will it find a new home in a world where it does not belong? A book about the **unconditional love between a parent and a child**, even if they are not biologically related.

Letters From Galaxy 8

The last of his kind, Nate must find a way to save his dying planet. He befriends Will from Earth. Can the two friends save Nate's world? A **space adventure** about **friendship** an the importance of **protecting our planet.**

Not Like The Others

250 forest animals! 17 children! 1 message about **diversity and inclusion**! Discover that we are all similar yet the same and that **it is our differences that make us special!**

Read-Alouds:

SCAN ME

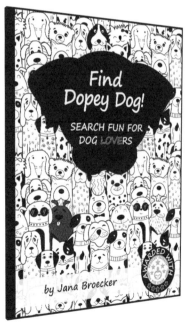

Coming Soon:

The Greedy King & The Kind Knight
A fairytale about kindness & integrity.

Pooperhero
A laugh-out-loud adventure about a healthy diet.

The Secret Ingredient
A cooking adventure about an unlikely friendship.

For the dog lover in your life

Find Dopey Dog!
Search Fun For Dog Lovers Of All Ages

Only one **Dopey Dog** hides in each of the beautifully illustrated **dog doodles**. Who can spot it first? Sounds easy, but gets **FUR**y complicated soon. **PAW**some fun for dog lovers of all ages.

You have loCATed the end
of this deliCATe book.
I hope you enjoyed it!

04fca117-ccd8-4d89-9e20-f7f959a24d99R01